In Search of Self-Governance

Scott W. Rasmussen

Rasmussen Reports, LLC
Asbury Park, New Jersey 07712

ISBN: 1-4495-9354-2
ISBN-13: 9781449593544

❖ ❖ ❖

Table of Contents

❖   ❖   ❖

Preface

As a public opinion pollster, I am often called upon to point out the differences between Americans—who supports this candidate or opposes that legislation. Which demographic group says yes, which says no?

And, of course, there are real differences to talk about. From a partisan perspective, Republican voters see things differently from Democrats. There are also differences between men and women, rich and poor, young and old, whites and non-whites, investors and non-investors, liberals and conservatives, government employees and entrepreneurs.

The more you divide America into subgroups, the more we seem divided.

Despite these differences, I am far more interested in what unites us. And, the good news is that there is lots of common ground that unites the American people today.

Like most Americans, I consider myself very fortunate to live in the United States. I'm proud to be an American and proud of our great national heritage—a heritage built upon freedom, liberty, and the belief that the people should rule their rulers. I am grateful for those who have given their lives defending our freedoms and thankful for those who defend us still today. While our nation is not perfect, the United States is more than a great place to live; it's a bright beacon of liberty and hope for the entire world.

Sadly, another piece of common ground today is frustration with political dialogue that seems designed to polarize and divide the public. Most of us have come to believe that the political system is broken, that most politicians are corrupt, and that neither major political party has the answers. Some of us are ready to give up and some of us are ready to scream a little louder. But all of us believe we can do better.

Dealing with a broken political system is especially frustrating because our nation has such a rich heritage of self-governance. The American people may disagree vehemently about specific policy issues, but we share a common belief that things work best when the people are in charge.

And that's why I wrote this essay. Self-governance is about far more than politics and government. It requires a lot of the American people and it has nothing to do with the petty partisan games played by Republicans and Democrats. Unfortunately, even after more than 200 years of success, there is now an urgent need to defend this most basic of American values.

This essay is not filled with polling data, but the ideas and attitudes presented are shared by a solid majority of Americans. In many ways, it is a celebration of consensus. Not everybody will agree with every single detail, but the overwhelming majority shares a deep commitment to *self*-governance.

That's what makes our nation special.

Scott W. Rasmussen

January 2010

❖ ❖ ❖

Part I

In Search of Self-Governance

❖　❖　❖

Conceived in Liberty

Following Barack Obama's election, Democrats and liberals believed that voters were looking to be governed from the left side of the political center. The only question for Democrats was how far left the center had moved.

Republicans and conservatives vehemently disagreed and claimed that the U.S. was still a center-right nation. Especially after the votes were counted in November, 2009, they debated whether Americans wanted to be governed from the center or by conservative values.

Both perspectives are wrong. The American people don't want to be governed from the left, the right, or the center.

The American people want to govern themselves.

In fact, they have been governing themselves for hundreds of years, continue to do so today, and will continue to do so for the foreseeable future. That's true regardless of whether Republicans or Democrats are running the show in Washington, DC.

The American attachment to self-governance runs deep. It is one of our nation's cherished core values and an important part of our cultural DNA. Self-governance is so completely ingrained in us that we take it for granted and hardly ever stop to think about it.

On holidays and during public rituals, we recite familiar and important words extolling the virtues of self-governance. But those words were written long ago, we have said them all a thousand times, and our bland delivery often robs those phrases of their majesty and power.

How often do we really stop and think about what it means to say that our nation was founded on the belief that we are all "created equal and endowed by [our] Creator with certain unalienable Rights." Those rights include "Life, Liberty, and the pursuit of Happiness" and convey an understanding of self-governance that embraces far more than just politics, government and voting.

Schoolchildren learn that our nation was "conceived in Liberty, and dedicated to the proposition that all men are created equal." Abraham Lincoln ended the most famous Presidential address of all time by calling for our nation to have a "new birth of freedom" so that "government of the people, by the people, and for the people shall not perish from the earth."

Today, in the twenty-first century, we don't often think about the virtues of self-governance Instead, we live them. Our society and daily life is still based upon those concepts so eloquently articulated long ago.

We give each and every individual the authority to make the most important decisions of all, the decisions about one's own life, one's family, one's faith, and one's job.

On matters that extend to the community, Americans get together with friends and neighbors and do what it takes to create a better place to live. More than 175 year ago, Alexis de Tocqueville learned this basic truth after coming to the United States seeking "the image of democracy itself."

The observant Frenchman noted that when something needed to be done, Americans got together with their neighbors to form community groups for everything from entertainment to distributing books, building churches, and beyond. In his words, "Americans of all ages, conditions, and dispositions constantly form associations...of a thousand kinds."

To us, that seems natural. Of course parents volunteer to help run Little League. Of course people volunteer at the soup kitchen or help build a Habitat House. But, to de Tocqueville, this American trait was radically different from the world he knew. In France or England, he observed, when something needed to be done, the government or a person of noble rank would be *asked* to do it.

Now, nearly two centuries later, Americans continue to form associations that make life better for all of us by getting involved and generously giving of time, talent, and treasure. More than 50 million of us volunteer each year for everything from churches, synagogues, sports teams, and civic clubs to environmental protection, education, and public safety efforts. And that doesn't begin to count the informal volunteering to help friends and neighbors when they need it.

This incredible level of civic involvement restores and refreshes our freedom and democracy on a daily basis. It has made our country great and it separates us from countries that rely on government or society's elites to make things happen.

In this context, it becomes clear that the daily choices made by individual Americans are more than individual acts of liberty. They are acts of self-governance that pass on values, raise children, help neighbors, build communities, and create a better quality of life for us all. That's how we built a great society that remains a beacon of liberty and hope throughout the world.

Today, despite that great legacy, the concept of self-governance gets no respect. Most Americans live it but don't acknowledge it.

Among the nation's political and corporate elites, it's even worse.

In the clique that revolves around Washington, DC and Wall Street, our treasured heritage has been diminished almost beyond recognition. In that world, some see self-governance as little more than allowing voters to choose which of two politicians will rule over them. Others in that elite environment are even more brazen and see self-governance as a problem to be overcome.

That elite view is a dangerous perspective.

A healthier perspective is to recognize that self-governance encompasses every aspect of life and every institution of society. We are all governed by many things and many people. At the same time, we all play a role in governing others.

That's the perspective that made America great. If we continue to embrace it, that perspective will also insure that America's best days are still in the future.

❖ ❖ ❖

Self-Governance in Daily Life

Most of us don't feel like we are governing our lives on a day-to-day basis. Many times, we feel lucky just to keep up with an overloaded calendar of commitments. Racing from meeting to meeting, answering cell phones, responding to e-mails, hurrying to school plays and PTA's, the few decisions we get to make sometimes involve little more than deciding whether to grab a sandwich before or after the next event.

Of course, those overcommitted days result from choices we've made before: choices about school, jobs, finances, housing, community commitments, social obligations, spouse, kids, friends, and more. The list could go on and on.

Those decisions, in turn, are driven by the values we choose to live by. Those who value money or power or fame will end up making different life choices than those who value family or faith or country. At different times in our lives, our own values and priorities are likely to change. In a self-governing society, that's okay. In fact, it's expected.

The beauty of self-governance is that we get to choose both our values and the way we implement them. What's the right mix between work and family, nurturing and disciplining our children, volunteering at church or spending time with your spouse? In Disney shows, the right choice is always clear. In real life, it's not.

In practical terms, we end up implementing our values one decision at a time by working our way through a complex maze of personal relationships, business entities, government rules, and voluntary associations.

Along the way, we get some things right and we also make our full share of mistakes. We learn from all of them—good decisions and bad—and we also learn from our friends and neighbors. That process—the things we get right, the mistakes we make, the opportunities we grab, and the dreams we let go by—creates consequences that govern the next steps of our journey. And, as much as we hate to admit it, consequences are just as much a part of self-governance as choices.

In fact, self-governance would be impossible without consequences to govern our decisions and our actions.

❖   ❖   ❖

Helping Govern Others

Our actions not only have consequences for our own lives, but they play a significant role in governing others. Once again, this is something we rarely think about or recognize.

One of the easiest places to see this at work is in the marketplace.

A self-governing society puts consumers in charge to rule the fate of entrepreneurs and corporations alike. When an entrepreneur meets an emerging need, the business grows. When consumers give thumbs down to the product line, even a once-mighty corporate giant like General Motors can't survive as an independent business.

In the Internet era, consumers drove start-ups like Yahoo! and AOL to dizzying heights. Later, when their needs were met better somewhere else, consumers forced both companies to stumble. If Yahoo! and AOL come back, it will be because they change what they do in a way to better meet consumer needs.

One of the great things about all this is that consumers don't have to get involved in the headaches of management to help govern these business challenges. We simply have to frequent those that meet our needs and avoid those that don't.

Having said all that, we rarely feel like we're governing businesses by acting as a consumer. When things go smoothly, we hardly think about it at all. We click and buy; the product shows up on time and in one piece. We buy a book and enjoy reading it.

But, when things go wrong, we can't seem to get the sales person or customer service rep to pay any attention to us and the managers are busy hiding. How can that happen if we're really helping to govern that underperforming business?

At one level, a visceral level, we don't feel like we're a governing factor because our mental image of governance is wrong. We picture government officials telling people what to do or the biggest bully on the playground beating our lunch money out of us.

But governance does not mean not acting like a diva and forcing people to scurry around in response to our latest whim. Sure, screaming and hollering sometimes gets things done, at least in the short-term. For some people, it might even make them feel good. But that approach typically buys cooperation at a pretty steep price.

Getting people to act in their own self-interest usually provides a longer-lasting impact.

Our real power as consumers comes not from being able to act like a diva and demand attention; it comes from the fact that businesses have to live with the consequences of the way they treat us. It's the "he who laughs last, laughs longest" kind of power. And, those companies that serve customers best end up making the most money.

When we enjoy a new restaurant and go back again, we are sending a positive signal to that business. When we bring friends with us and tell others about it, that's even more positive.

On the other hand, when we're treated rudely at a department store and don't go back, that's a different kind of signal. When we tell our friends about the shabby treatment we received at that store, the signal grows stronger.

These signals from consumers are the most powerful force in the world when it comes to governing the behavior of companies. Similar signals work at every level of legitimate transactions. Companies that treat their employees well are able to attract more applicants. That means they can hire the employees who will do the best job of serving customers.

In a properly functioning society, treating people well is good business. You prosper by serving others. It's also common sense and an obvious benefit of the free-market system.

But, it doesn't seem much like self-governance. At least not until we think of how these actions govern society at large.

In a healthy and properly functioning society, companies that serve their customers well will grow and prosper. Those that don't will either change their ways or shrink and disappear. Society benefits—we all benefit—because companies that provide good service get to serve more consumers.

At the same time, those companies that fail to meet the needs of consumers will impact an ever-shrinking share of the marketplace.

Sometimes, the process is painful to watch. These days, print newspapers are disappearing as consumers get more and more of their news and information online. For better or worse, consumers are craving different types of information and demanding it on a real-time basis. Newspapers are now struggling to make a comeback and figure out how to survive in an online world. Plenty of others will enter the fray to figure out how best to get consumers the information we need and want.

It's not at all clear how this will end up, how consumers will receive their news in a generation, or how they will pay for it. But it is clear that consumers are in charge. The eventual winners of the news industry will be selected by individuals making their own choices and letting others compete to serve them.

Consumers are also in charge when it comes to every other business in the nation, from the self-employed artist to giant companies that seem to dominate the landscape today. Big companies and big brand names don't last forever. It is hard to imagine, but—when consumers decide it's time—companies like Microsoft, Wal-Mart, Kraft Foods, UPS, and Google will all suffer the same fate as General Motors and Chrysler. Nothing lasts forever.

There will even come a day when they don't play the World Series or Super Bowl any more. That day will come when consumers (fans) decide they don't really care.

It's important to note that even our decisions as consumers have an impact far beyond the business world.

For example, we routinely make decisions about which church, synagogue, charitable, and community organizations to support with our time, our talents, and our treasure. This can be anything from buying Girl Scout cookies to taking a leadership role in a church project, drawing attention to government corruption, or highlighting a real community need.

Sometimes, our actions help those who took the initiative. Other times, our actions let them know that we don't share their enthusiasm for a charity project, their understanding of government corruption, or their opinion of real community needs.

But, always, our actions and decisions play a vital role in a self-governing society.

❖   ❖   ❖

How Our Opinions Govern Others

Our opinions also play a vital role. That's because reputations matter both to individuals and to organizations.

At the most basic level, the opinions of those we care about can have a powerful impact in terms of governing our own day-to-day behavior. What my wife thinks of me—and my actions—has a great deal of impact on what I do and the decisions I make. So do the opinions of my children, my pastor, and close friends. Generally, of course, this isn't much of an issue because we share underlying values and perceptions.

Still, at decision time, it's reassuring when those close to me confirm my perspective or judgment. When they don't, when their opinion differs from mine, that by itself is enough reason for me to pause and reconsider my actions.

And, like everything else in a free and self-governing society, the things that govern us also enable us to help govern others. So, while our behavior is often guided by the opinion of others, the reverse is just as true, our opinions can have a powerful impact on those we care about.

But, the power of individual opinions can also, in appropriate settings and circumstances, have an impact beyond our immediate circle of family and friends.

In every organization, our opinions help others learn who is easy to work with, who is a good leader, who is a good helper, who is a good mentor, who gets things done, and who to stay away from. Some people work well under pressure, others don't. Some never miss a deadline, others never meet one.

This information—passed along informally—does more than assess individuals; it helps get the right people in the right place at the right time so that the organization can get things done.

Taking the power of individual opinion a step further, Indiana Governor Mitch Daniels recently urged college graduates to "Please, *be judgmental.*"

To some twenty-first century ears, that very phrase will seem offensive. What gives us the right to pass judgment? Properly understood and properly exercised, however, being judgmental is an important part of self-governance.

Daniels explained that "As free people, we agree to tolerate any conduct that does no harm to others, but we should not be coerced into condoning it. Selfishness and irresponsibility in business, personal finances or in family life are deserving of your disapproval. Go ahead and stigmatize them. Too much of such behavior will hurt our nation."

He's right, of course.

It may be legal to collect millions of dollars after leading your company to a taxpayer bailout, but the rest of us don't have to approve of that behavior. And, as a society, it is legal to focus excessively on materialistic pursuits, but that doesn't mean we should embrace greed as our national purpose.

The gap between what is legal and what is acceptable plays a vitally important role in a self-governing society. This gap is where most of the work gets done to create a society that truly reflects the will of the American people.

❖ ❖ ❖

What about Politics and Government?

James Madison came of age when principles of self-governance were being discussed in ways that would change the world. He was 14 when the Stamp Act sparked colonial protests and 25 when those protests inspired the Declaration of Independence.

Thirty years old when the British surrendered to end the Revolutionary War, Madison was destined to play a great role in the founding of a new nation and a new form of government. He became the primary author of our nation's Constitution, helped write the influential *Federalist Papers,* and drafted the amendments known to history as the Bill of Rights. But he did more than write. Madison was a delegate to the Continental Congress, served in the first Congress of the United States, was Thomas Jefferson's Secretary of State, oversaw the Louisiana Purchase, and became the fourth President of the United States.

In short, James Madison did as much as any other man to design and build our nation's system of formal government.

Madison and his peers certainly hoped that a well-designed government might serve to "refine and enlarge the public views" on challenging issues. They gave a great deal of thought to how government could receive the appropriate consent of the governed without succumbing to the temporary passions of a mob.

But, while seeking to build a government, Madison never lost sight of the fact that the government was merely a means to an end. His objective was to create a self-governing society and the government was designed to serve that larger purpose.

The Founders created a system of checks and balances by providing separate branches of government with different tenures and constituencies—the House is elected for two-year terms, the President for four, the Senate for six and the Supreme Court gets to serve for life. House members are elected from a District, Senators from a State, and the President from an Electoral College.

That framework—rooted in common sense—creates headaches for those in power. With different constituencies, different terms, and different roles for different offices, it's not very efficient.

In fact, when you look at the checks and balances in our Constitution from the perspective of politicians trying to get things done, it just doesn't seem to make much sense. More than 200 years later, Presidents and Congress still grumble about how hard it is to bring about change in the Madisonian system.

That's okay, because our government wasn't designed to serve the needs of those in power. It was designed to support a self-governing society. In fact, the headaches for politicians are better than okay because they're precisely what Madison and his peers had in mind.

Bob Dove, who recently served as Senate parliamentarian for more than a decade, put it this way: "The U.S. Senate is designed to keep bad laws from passing." In words that would make Madison proud, Dove said the Senate "is a check on the House, on the President, on the public. It is difficult to get a bill passed into law, and it is supposed to be."

By making it difficult for politicians to get things done quickly, the Founders created a mechanism that would force society to reach a consensus before major new programs were launched.

The need to build support for programs over time and across a variety of constituencies was an important part of maintaining the "consent of the governed" that gives government its legitimacy. Senator Daniel Patrick Moynihan recognized the same principle when he said "Never pass major legislation that affects most Americans without real bipartisan support. It opens the door to all kinds of political trouble."

Building support over time provides protection against the temporary passions of the mob because a single election could never change control of all branches of government. The system of checks and balances also provided protection against granting excessive power to the government without broad societal support.

In designing that system, Madison recognized something that just about everybody in Washington tries to forget. The government does not run the country. It is one institution among many that makes a self-governing society work.

❖ ❖ ❖

Does Self-Governance Really Work?

Most Americans can easily accept the notion that people get to govern their own lives and that their actions help govern those around them. People instinctively know that doing volunteer service work in the community is more important than getting wrapped up in politics and political campaigns.

If they ever stopped to think about it, most would also recognize that this is what the founders of the country had in mind. Most share the view that that in a healthy society, government will play a supporting role rather than taking the lead.

But, despite all that, some people have a hard time believing that this sort of self-governance can stand up to the enormous power of government. They have nagging doubts about whether individuals and community groups and neighbors can really bring about the kind of change that America needs. It's hard to let go of the storyline, coming out of Washington, that elections determine the fate of the nation.

And that leads to discouragement and pessimism. Those who fear that only government action can bring about the needed change get depressed because our political system is so badly broken.

Fortunately, however, a self-governing society typically works well enough to pick up the slack from what the political system can't get done.

One way to see this principle in action is to take a look at the Social Security debate.

As everybody knows, the New Deal's most popular program faces enormous financial pressures. To solve the problem, countless politicians have talked about countless solutions—everything from hiking taxes or upping the retirement age to cutting benefits and making the program voluntary. But, despite lots of ideas and plenty of time to work on them, the political world has failed to come up with a solution.

Fortunately, the American people have been dealing with the reality before them for years rather than waiting for somebody else.

The first thing to notice about the way self-governing individuals are solving the problem is that they are not focused on the political issue of Social Security. They are focused on the more important matters of life, including planning for life after age 65. What will it be like? What are the options?

For most working age Americans, that means things like sitting down with financial planners and setting up retirement plans and 401(k) accounts. It means accepting the reality that Social Security will eventually be forced to change and making plans for getting by in retirement without it.

That's a healthy and pragmatic approach: If we get our benefits, great, it's a bonus. If we get some of our benefits, that's okay, too. What if we don't get any? Well, we weren't counting on the benefits to begin with and we're prepared.

This approach means a lot of hard work. Setting aside money for retirement is a challenge when you're raising a family. It's especially hard when we have to pay 12% of our income off the top to cover Social Security benefits promised for today's retirees. But, that's what we have to do, so we do it.

Some people are good at this, and some try hard. But all find solutions. For some it might involve cutting back a bit on expenses while others work past age 65. Some will work because they weren't able to set aside enough money along the way and some because their 401(k) isn't what it once was.

Others don't need the money but work because they don't want to retire. That perspective is one the policy wonks never expected. In fact, it caused a recent shock to the political system when a protest emerged from older workers who were penalized for going back to work. That's just one of many examples that show how millions of Americans are finding their own path in response to the realities before them.

To those who want bold legislative accomplishments, these steps may seem petty and insignificant. In reality, the pragmatism of the American people is addressing two issues that the political world can't handle.

First, the pragmatism about retirement is addressing questions of life and work after 65 in a way that rejects the one-size-fits-all solution. Some people can't wait to retire early, others can't imagine waking up without something to work on. Some retire and devote time to church or synagogue and charity; others travel the world and play. There is no right or wrong answer; there are only choices.

Second, by preparing for their own retirement, today's generation of workers will make Social Security less essential in the future. This contribution should not be underestimated as we cover the cost of promises made long-ago to today's retirees while at the same time preparing for our own retirement.

Social Security benefits will eventually become a bonus during retirement, something extra that we can have a little fun with. When we accomplish that goal, it will be much easier for politicians to deal with the remaining issues of financing Social Security.

By being pragmatic and addressing the retirement issue one-by-one, this generation of workers will give a priceless gift to future generations. We will be the sandwich generation and pay for two generations worth or retirement—our own and our parents. Because we are doing this, future generations won't have to do the same.

Later, after the American people have done their work, the formal governing bodies can come along and ratify the change that society has made possible. We don't know what the final legislative package will look like or what form Social Security might take a century from now. What we do know is that the American people will provide the framework for change long before the politicians enact the needed reform.

So, while it's easy to get discouraged about what we watch in the political sphere, we shouldn't make the mistake of assuming that the politicians hold the fate of the nation in their hands. A self-governing society can recover from the mistakes of politicians.

The reason it works is simple. Even though our political system is badly broken, our society is generally fair and decent. Self-governance works even when politics and government do not.

That's the way it's always been in America.

In 1963, Birmingham's Public Safety Commissioner Bull Conner was aggressively enforcing and promoting laws requiring racial segregation. In a notorious moment aired on national television, Conner's people turned fire hoses on well dressed black children in prayer. While Conner saw those children as threats to law and order, most Americans disagreed. They were horrified and judgmental—Conner was stigmatized as a symbol of bigotry.

Conner's moment in the national spotlight came after years of activity that highlighted the reality of government-imposed segregation throughout the South. As the then-new technology of television made that reality visible to millions of Americans, the era of official segregation came to an end.

While Congress eventually passed Civil Rights Acts in the mid-1960s, it's important to realize that it was the decisions and opinions of millions of individual Americans that brought segregation to an end. The legal and legislative steps that followed simply ratified the decision already reached by a self-governing society.

That's the kind of solution that our Founding Fathers anticipated and hoped for because it's what they themselves experienced.

During the decades before 1776, opinions about the proper relationship between the 13 American colonies and England changed dramatically. Americans, living on the other side of the Atlantic, developed very different understandings than those living in England. Some even began to think of the American colonies as a separate nation.

However, in England, the view emerged that the Americans weren't paying their fair share of taxes. To the leaders in London, the very least the colonies should do was pay for the cost of their own defense.

The colonists, however, had adopted a view that the British soldiers were occupiers, not protectors. Being told that they had pay higher taxes to support the occupying force struck many colonists as the last straw. That led to the rallying cry of "No Taxation without Representation."

Across the Atlantic, that made little sense. The English Parliament operated under a theory of virtual representation which held that members of Parliament represented all citizens of the Empire. In London, they believed the colonists were represented. But, to the colonists, representation meant having the chance to elect one of their own.

More than anything specific, it was these fundamentally different perceptions developed over decades that made the American Revolution possible and perhaps inevitable. As John Adams put it, "The Revolution was won before a single shot was fired. The real revolution was in the hearts and minds of the American people."

Having seen the reality of what a self-governing society could accomplish in practice, the founders of our nation sought to create a system that would allow it to thrive for generations.

❖ ❖ ❖

Part II

The Threat to Self-Governance

❖ ❖ ❖

An Unholy Alliance

Despite our great heritage, the continuation of the United States as a self-governing society is far from assured. In fact, quite the opposite is true. In these early days of the 21st century, our system of self-governance is in trouble.

We are in danger of becoming a nation where big business and big government work together against the rest of us. They write the rules, we pay the bills. And then they wonder why we get upset.

It is painfully easy to see how far we have already fallen.

In a self-governing society, businesses make money when they serve customers and go out of business when they don't. Consumers frequent the businesses that meet their needs and avoid those that don't. Community organizations that truly fill a need attract the resources and volunteers to keep going. Some churches and synagogues grow, and some disappear.

In 21st century America, small businesses, churches, charitable organizations, and ordinary citizens still play by those rules. But, most large companies don't.

The largest and best-connected companies keep the profits when they succeed and get bailed out by the government when they fail. Either way, win or lose, the top executives at large publicly-traded companies draw salaries that look meager only in comparison to the bills taxpayers receive for the bailouts.

This unholy alliance between the largest corporations and the government is a natural and inevitable result of moving away from a national commitment to self-governance.

Bit by bit, over a century and a half or so, the largest corporations have been chipping away at the bonds of accountability that came from having to serve customers. In an era with growing stock ownership among the middle class, elite managers of publicly traded companies have also managed to get protection from their investors. In far too many cases, that protection has let corporate managers reap huge rewards while stockholders have seen the value of their investment dwindle.

At the same time, politicians have been chipping away at the system of checks and balances developed by our Founding Fathers. The rules of the election game have been written to put third parties at a disadvantage while giving incumbent politicians enormous advantages over anybody who would dare challenge them.

As a result, the gap today between Americans who want to govern themselves and politicians who want to rule over them may be as big as the gap between the colonies and England during the 18th century. And that's true whether Republicans or Democrats are in charge.

The fact that politicians in both parties are out of synch with a nation that wants to govern itself is one reason that neither party has been able to hang on to power in recent decades. Since World War II, with only one exception, neither political party has held on to the White House for more than eight years at a time. Prior to World War II, the norm was for one party to dominate the White House for long stretches of time.

Now, it's been more than 40 years since a President left office with his party in control of Congress. Nobody has governed well enough to win a Presidential landslide victory since 1984. In earlier times, such agenda confirming landslides occurred with regularity.

And the signs are getting even more ominous. Both President Bill Clinton and President George W. Bush entered office with their party having majority control of Congress. Both managed to lose control before their Administration came to an end. Never before in our nation's history has that happened in back-to-back Administrations.

Voters have become disillusioned and don't believe anybody in power is listening to them. As 2008 turned into 2009, voters overwhelmingly opposed the bailout of the financial industry and the extension of the bailouts to the auto industry. Despite the overwhelming public consensus against bailouts, the Bush Administration, the Obama Administration and most of official Washington never gave it a second thought.

To many voters, it appeared as if the government was more interested in maintaining Wall Street profits than in creating a financial system that works for the rest of us. Adding insult to injury is the perception that most of the taxpayer money went to bail out the very people who created the problem in the first place.

The only good news is that while the nation's political system appears to be breaking down, the American people continue to do the hard work of self-governance. They take responsibility for the decisions that affect them and they continue to do the things that make communities work.

While it's good that most Americans recognize that these activities are more important than politics, there is an unfortunate side effect.

Large segments of the population—people from all walks of life and all points of view—are now completely turned off by politics and disgusted by politicians. Shock rocker Alice Cooper, whose classic anthem "School's Out" once captured the mood of school children everywhere, more recently captured the national mood concerning politics: "When I was a kid and my parents started talking about politics, I'd run to my room and put on the Rolling Stones as loud as I could."

While Cooper is now 60-something and more likely to flee to the golf course than listen to the Stones, he is not alone. Many people who do the hard work of self-governance have withdrawn from any significant involvement in the political realm. They are repulsed by the anger, mean spirit, and rudeness of political "dialogue."

Besides, given the choice, who wouldn't rather spend time with family or friends? Who wouldn't rather work on a community project where you can really make a difference and have an impact? But if America is to retain its heritage as a self-governing society, we can't completely avoid the political system just because it is broken, because it is less important, or because we find the topic distasteful.

People who believe in self-governance should occasionally get involved in politics for the same reason we occasionally get involved with Little League: to provide adult supervision. That means doing more than just cheering for our favorite political team. We need to set the ground rules and provide a little perspective.

In Little League, the adults often remind players that there are far more important things in life than winning or losing a particular game.

In politics, that means reminding politicians that they have authority only as long as they retain the "consent of the governed." They work for the voters, not the other way around.

This is where it becomes difficult. The hostile environment of 21st century politics means that the very people who could be the best chaperones are reluctant to get involved and provide the adult supervision that America's politicians so desperately need.

That's just fine with those in the world professional politics. They want meaningful citizen involvement about as much as mischievous teenagers want chaperones at a high school dance.

Actually, it's even worse than that.

Imagine what it might be like if the teens decided what kind of behavior was acceptable at the dance and placed limits on what the chaperones could do about it. That's how it works in Washington today. And, again, it's not because Democrats are in charge or because Republicans are in charge. It's the way both parties play the game.

That's why just electing one political team instead of the other isn't enough to bring about real change.

Rather than just switching between Republicans and Democrats from time to time, real change will require turning the political world upside down. We need to put the chaperones back in charge.

❖　❖　❖

A Big Hill to Climb

To understand how much work needs to be done, consider the humorous and amazingly Washington-centric perspective once offered by a U.S. Senator: "The ballot box is the place where all change begins in America." Apparently, he never heard of Steve Jobs or Bill Gates!

Throughout American history, entrepreneurs like Alexander Graham Bell have brought about change without getting approval from Congress or the voters. Henry Ford invented the assembly line on his own in Michigan. Ray Kroc built the McDonald's fast food chain by enforcing quality standards and selling franchises rather than running a political campaign. The list of entrepreneurs who changed America could go on and on.

That entrepreneurial spirit is one reason government works best in a supporting role rather than the lead role.

This reality doesn't diminish official Washington's mistaken assessment of its own place in the center of the known universe. *The Politico* once reported that a legislative debate would be determined "less by the intelligence of advocates on any side than by the ignorance of most Americans."

Further reflecting the bi-partisan views of its elite audience, the article added, "It may go too far to say that Americans are too dumb to understand." *May go too far? May?* According to the article, the challenge for the politicians is "How to boil down arguments...into simple appeals that will engage an easily distracted, easily flustered electorate."

Think about that for a moment. The people who live off the taxpayers think we're too dumb to understand what they do. I guess that's why the folks in DC don't think too much about government of the people, by the people, and for the people.

Just to be clear, *The Politico* is a great publication that serves its audience very well. That's what makes those statements so stunning. They accurately reflect the condescending view that official Washington holds towards the rest of us.

The Politico is not alone in capturing this Washington-centric attitude held by the nation's political and corporate elites. A *Washington Post* writer opined that the challenge for DC leaders is how to "harness the energy" of their party's base voters while not allowing them "to grab the steering wheel."

Adam Nagourney once wrote in *The New York Times* blog that "It's going to be awfully hard to avoid President Obama on television this Sunday." Why? According to Nagourney, it was because "The president is going to appear on five Sunday talk shows...That is a presidential record."

In reality, of course, only about 3% of Americans watch those Sunday morning shows, so it would be easy for most of us to miss the President completely. But, it's probably true that everybody who matters to the DC crowd was watching, even if most of the nation was busy with more productive pursuits.

❖ ❖ ❖

Sports Bar Nation

Many things that official Washington finds fascinating are hardly even noticed outside the halls of power. For most Americans, the political world is background noise, an annoyance, or non-existent.

It's true, of course, that some people outside the Beltway spend a considerable amount of time and energy talking about that background noise. Their comments fill talk radio shows, blogs, and other forums. It makes politicians feel that they are leading a great national debate. But if you listen carefully, most political talk sounds just like sports talk. Political fans cheer for their team while trash-talking the other. They typically preach to their own choir or shout past the other team's fans without listening.

Some Americans passionately want the Yankees to beat the Red Sox. Others passionately want one politician to beat another. For millions, politics has simply become another spectator sport. Politically, we have become a sports bar nation.

In today's world, both sets of teams even come complete with home team announcers, team colors and mascots. Are you from a Red State or a Blue State? Donkey or Elephant? When one game ends, the next begins. And, just like all good sporting events, the results can all be found instantly just by visiting the internet.

And, let's face it; the sport of politics is sometimes great fun. But it's rarely of great impact.

When the fun is over, and the political games are turned off, most Americans get back to the hard, daily work of self-governance. We provide for our families, work with neighbors to create a better community, act as consumers, and voice our opinions in a healthy manner.

Unfortunately, some people are so wrapped up in politics that they don't have time for the work of self-governance. For them, the competition never ends. They never take time away from politics to fulfill their basic responsibilities in a self-governing society. Rather than volunteering to help a community event, they spend their time shilling for yet another candidate.

Many political activists get so caught up in the competition that they act as if the fate of the world hinges on the results of the next election. As they see it, things will be unspeakably bad unless their candidate wins. That leads to a win-at-all-cost mentality which produces a hate-filled undercurrent every election season.

During Election 2008, I was swamped with hateful e-mails from fans of John McCain. Why? They were angry and accused me of bias because my polls consistently showed Barack Obama with a solid lead. I got the same reaction from Hillary Clinton fans, Mike Huckabee fans, and Mitt Romney fans during the 2008 Primary Campaign when their heroes weren't doing so well in the polls. Ron Paul fans were in a league of their own and John Kerry fans did the same back in 2004.

The vitriol in all those e-mails was stunning and it didn't matter which side sent them. If we showed one side going up in the polls, the other side would unleash a volley of hate. If we showed the other side going up, we got essentially the same letters and the only thing that changed were the names of the candidates we were allegedly helping or hurting.

Depending upon who was writing and what their complaint was, people wanted to know how much I got from selling my soul to George Soros and MoveOn.org or to Fox News and the Bush Administration.

Some were simply long strings of what an earlier political generation would refer to as Expletive Deleted. Others questioned my integrity, my ancestry, my credibility, and often offered "proof" that I was obviously biased in favor of either the Republicans or the Democrats.

In 2004 and heading into 2010, most of the complaints came from the political left because things were not going in their direction. In 2006 and 2008, most of the complaints came from the right for the same reason.

It all sounded just like the comments you'd hear about referees in a football game. One set of fans would say a particular call was a no-brainer while the other side would say the ref was blind, biased, or out of his mind. And, of course, rabid fans of either sports or politics sometimes voice their opinions in very colorful language.

The hate and anger that dominates in political circles is clear evidence that activists and fans have lost their sense of perspective. They have forgotten that there are far more important things in our national life than which politician wins a particular election.

The truth is that politicians aren't nearly as important as they think they are. Most progress in our nation originates far outside the halls of Congress and most of the ideas that have made our country great come from people who have a life outside of politics. Besides, no politician will ever be as good as his or her fans hope and none will ever be as bad as his or her opponents fear.

And, if one politician strays too far away from reality, the checks and balances that Madison created will provide some damage control. But the bigger protection comes from the fact that what we do in our day-to-day lives is more important than what politicians do in legislatures.

Just like in Little League, it may still hurt when your political team loses. But it's not the end of the world.

Does It Matter Who Represents Your District in Congress?

Political activists routinely snicker about the fact that most Americans can't even name their own representative in Congress. To political junkies, who view these elected politicians as princes or petty monarchs, this is a sure sign of public ignorance. From a different perspective, it's a bit like not knowing the names of the cool kids in junior high school.

But, like junior high students worried about hanging with the cool kids, political activists are so wrapped up in their own world that they miss a very basic point—there's no reason that most people should know who represents their district in Congress. It might help in a game of Trivial Pursuit, but what difference does it make in the real world?

Knowing the name of your District's rep in Congress is certainly not going to give you any influence over how that person acts or votes. Unless you're a close friend, lobbyist, or big donor, they're not going to pick up the phone when you call.

And if you need help from a Congressional office, you don't need to know the Congressman's name. Congress has set up a web service where you can enter your zip code and they'll connect you with the appropriate office staff. All legislators are happy to help, especially since the constituent services are paid for by taxpayers.

What about elections and voting? Well, about 90% of Americans live in Congressional Districts specifically designed to avoid competitive races and offer no meaningful choice to voters. Incumbents like it that way. But, if there's no meaningful choice, knowing the name of your representative doesn't matter even on Election Day.

Activists from both political parties like to discourage talk about the way elections are essentially rigged for one party or the other. They tend to trot out the tired cliché that "voters hate Congress but love their own Congressman." They intentionally overlook the obvious contradiction that people can't love their elected officials if they don't know their name. Deep down, they know the truth. Legislators win re-election for the same reason that casinos make money: they write the rules.

Still, there are a handful of voters who live in a place with a competitive race. Is it important for them to know the name of their District's rep? Not really. There's no avoiding the campaign commercials and other campaign pollution leading up to Election Day. And there is plenty of time to get the relevant facts on the candidates and the partisan dynamics in the weeks before casting a vote. That lets us do our duty, vote, and then return to the important work of self-governance.

Despite the misplaced priorities of the political pros, there is no particular reason for most people to memorize the name of their district's elected politician. In a world filled with information overload, there are far more important things to remember. Besides, if members of Congress were connected to the community as they should be, we would know more than their names.

That statement may be close to heresy for those who view members of Congress as the rightful rulers of the nation. But, it's really nothing more than a healthy perspective for a self-governing society. And correcting Washington's perspective is what will turn the world of politics upside down.

Free Markets Versus Big Business

Correcting Washington's perspective on the importance of politics and politicians is only one part of the challenge before advocates of self-governance.

It is also important to take a fresh look at the relationship between big business, free markets, and government.

As currently presented by the political gang in Washington, the story line goes something like this: Big government and big business are perpetual and intractable enemies. Big business wants totally free and unfettered markets while big government wants to regulate everything that moves. Democrats tend to line up with big government but some are more moderate and also consider business perspectives. Republicans tend to line up with big business but some are more moderate and also recognize the need for government involvement.

As the story goes, the two sides duke it out and end up with compromise regulations. Businesses get enough freedom to compete while government gets enough regulation to protect consumers.

This is bunk!

The reality is a bit like a scam you'd see in a bad movie. Some guy is harassing a girl at a bar and another guy steps in to chase the jerk away. For good measure, he gets tough and just a little bit physical.

After the jerk is gone, the "hero" is free to accept whatever thanks he can from the damsel who thought she was in distress. She, of course, has no way of knowing that the two guys were friends and will switch roles the next time they try the scam.

In the political world today, advocates of big business and big government play the same game. They pretend to fight so that one of them can rise to the defense of consumers or taxpayers. Big business leaders proclaim the virtues of the free market and regulators talk about a mandate to protect consumers. Just as the guys reverse roles when it suits them, the elites take turns drifting back and forth between the business and government sides of the aisle.

Over the last couple of years, these phony fights have paid off big time. Businesses have been bailed out with hundreds of billions of dollars of taxpayer money and government officials get to run banks and auto companies. What's not to love?

There is a simple reason that things turned out so badly for taxpayers in this arrangement. It's what always happens when government and big business work together.

A generation ago, Savings and Loan companies were freed to make risky investments and keep the profits when they worked. But, when the investments didn't work out, the government wrote the rules so that taxpayers got stuck with a tab that reached hundreds of billions of dollars.

The same thing happens at state and local levels when governments make special deals to get businesses to locate on one side of the border or the other. Regardless of the state or city, the politicians get the ribbon cutting ceremony and the taxpayers get the bill.

The alliance between government and big business works largely because the players have been quite successful at selling the false notion that they really are political opponents. Once they do that, they story line flows naturally to suggest that the only options are a choice between government regulation and no regulation. That's a phony choice.

As noted earlier, all of us are governed by the actions of others and all that we do helps to govern others. The real question, the one the phony fight obscures, is whether the key decisions that control the fate of corporations are made by consumers or government officials.

Given that choice, the nation's largest public corporations would almost always prefer the manageable regulation from a government official. Truly free markets are terrifying to most big businesses because they cannot be controlled or managed. Even the largest corporation with the biggest marketing budget can't make up for poor performance and survive when smaller and more innovative competitors are preferred by consumers.

But, large companies can buy protection from the wrath of consumers if they put their money into lobbying rather than customer service. Such protection is often easy to find when the regulators are part of the same crowd who routinely drift back and forth between government and the corporate world.

And, the moment corporations begin to focus on pleasing government officials rather than consumers, one of the key controls of a self-governing society breaks down. That's why even the best-sounding regulations implemented with the purest of intentions can end up doing more harm than good.

Consumers acting in a free market will always provide tougher oversight than government officials. If consumers had been allowed to determine the fate of Citibank, AIG, General Motors, and other bailed out companies, those companies would no longer exist.

And, by the way, the executive bonuses that were eventually paid by the taxpayers wouldn't have even been considered if consumers had let the companies fail.

Anything that causes companies to worry more about what regulators will say than what consumers will do weakens the public oversight of corporate America.

It's clear why those corporations prefer the protection of government regulators. It's just as clear why it's better for everybody else to have consumers in charge.

And, it should be noted, it's not just a question of saving taxpayer dollars. It's a question of basic fairness. Why should corporations be allowed to profit when they succeed and be bailed out when they don't? Why should government officials have the right to determine which failing companies are deemed worthy of bailing out?

The fact that government officials have such power is the reason it has become so lucrative for executives to move back and forth between the private sector and government. It certainly didn't hurt Citibank to have a former Treasury Secretary in senior management when they were seeking a bailout. And the arrangement doesn't hurt the employment prospects of those who seek to cash in after a period of time as a government employee.

Having said all that, it is important to remember that there are many individuals in both government and large corporations who behave honorably and play by the rules. In fact, most are probably quite decent on a personal basis. The problem is that the rules of the game have been written in a way that cuts consumers and taxpayers out of the loop.

When the system is corrupt, it is not enough to have honorable people in power who play by the rules. Even the most honest business leader can be pressured to give campaign contributions because he fears members of Congress will help their friends and hurt their political opponents. Even the most conscientious regulator can fear for her career if she doesn't help powerful politicians assist their friends in the corporate suites.

The only way to fix this is to change the underlying rules of the game.

And the new rules need to apply to all of us. Politicians should not be allowed to use taxpayers' money to pick and choose who wins and who loses in America.

Just to be clear, free markets don't mean an unfettered *laissez-faire* capitalism where anything goes. That's a caricature put forth by those who like the status quo.

A healthy system will be a lot closer to something James Madison would structure rather than a recreation of the Wild West. As with almost everything else in a self-governing society, there is an important supporting role for government to play. But, it is a supporting role and one that should empower consumers rather than replace them.

When regulators are in charge, those who can game the system win. When consumers are in charge, those who serve the consumers win.

In a self-governing society, service to the consumer must be the driving force that determines success or failure for businesses. That lets the American people themselves select the winners and losers.

So, just as it's important to remember that Washington politics is not the source of all that happens in America, it's important to remember that a ghastly marriage of convenience between government and big business has those two allies working together against the rest of us.

❖   ❖   ❖

A Different Perspective

When missionaries prepare for a journey, one of the first steps is to study the culture they will visit. They need to understand the culture before they can understand how to connect with people who view the world from an entirely different perspective.

Those who want to provide adult supervision for America's politicians need to do the same. The place to begin is with the politicians themselves.

It's easy to dismiss politicians as self-centered, power-hungry, and hypocritical. And those, some might say, are the good ones!

It's especially easy to adopt that view when politicians have created a political environment that is so hostile to most Americans.

But, for those who are serious about defending self-governance, it's important to recognize that not all political activists and elected politicians are completely opposed to letting the American people govern themselves. Whenever they find time to think about it, many of these partisan professionals recognize the importance of entrepreneurs, civic organizations, and family. Unfortunately, such thoughts are quickly crowded out in the day-to-day turmoil of the political world.

On average, of course, professional politicians are more likely than the rest of us to see a leading role for government in society. If they didn't have that view, they would have chosen a different career. And, it must be noted that this trait applies to both liberal politicians and conservative politicians, Democrats and Republicans. Liberal politicians and conservative politicians may want to lead in different directions, but both want to lead rather than serve.

But, despite their faith in government, most elected politicians at least start their career with some respect for the basic concepts of self-governance. A fair number even got started in the political game because of their belief in self-governance.

Some may have even gotten involved to become chaperones but ended up getting sucked into playing the game.

Unfortunately, a lifetime of playing politics in Washington can bury just about anyone's belief in self-governance beneath a layer of political pragmatism and cynicism. Some players don't even try anymore and just sell out. Others have been playing the game so long that they can't remember anything else. Some are tired of fighting the activists and donors.

But even among those who have stayed in DC too long, not all have completely abandoned their positive instincts. Anything that we can do to awaken those instincts will be a step in right direction.

Think of it like Luke Skywalker working to retrieve the little bit of good left in Darth Vader.

In the *Star Wars* saga, Vader was seduced by the power of the dark side and sold out to the Emperor early in life. He tried to wipe out all who opposed him, including Luke. But Luke continued to fight the Empire and continued reaching out to Vader. In the biggest battle of all, Luke refused to play by the Emperor's rules and nearly died for his principles. But Luke's courage and example convinced Vader to turn back from the dark side and helped save the day.

Career politicians may have gone over to the dark side, but it's not too late for all of them.

How Are They Led Astray?

If we want to retrieve some of our political leaders and restore their commitment to self-governance, we should perhaps consider what led them astray in the first place.

Some voters believe that campaign contributions are the root of the problem. Others think that just hanging out in a company town like Washington for too long leads political types to forget where they came from. For others, the villain is the incessant and petty partisanship that forces politicians to focus only on the next election.

But all of these factors combined don't really explain what causes good citizens to drift away from a commitment to self-governance.

The core problem is that there are a few people on all sides of the ideological divide who really don't like the idea of self-governance. Some are liberals and some are conservatives, but they think that the government should run everything, or just about everything. Some of them may just like being in charge and bossing people around.

Whatever the reason, this ideologically diverse group envisions a system where the elites run the government and the government runs the nation. They trust the wisdom of their Ivy League friends more than they trust the wisdom of the crowd. That's a fundamental departure from more than two centuries of self-governance.

While the number holding such views is relatively small, they have a couple of tactical advantages in the political realm that create challenges for those who believe in self-governance.

First, people who believe government should be in charge naturally gravitate to government service. So, while it's hard to find anybody outside of politics and government who opposes self-governance, a scarily high percentage of policy makers are reluctant to let the people lead.

Second, those in government who favor rule by the elites can pursue that objective on a full-time paid basis. Their ideological interests, their passion for politics, and their career interests are closely aligned.

In an earlier time, these people would have been called the Tories. They were royalists who wanted the United States to remain loyal to the King and the British Empire.

Today, these royalists continue to challenge the basic premise of the American Revolution and the principles outlined in the Declaration of Independence.

The chaperones trying to oversee them are working on a volunteer basis after already fulfilling their primary self-governing responsibilities to family, job, and community. In terms of hours, energy level, and focus, it is clearly a mismatch, with the opponents of self-governance holding the advantage.

As a result, the minority who oppose self-governance find themselves in a position where they can greatly leverage their power and influence.

Let's be clear. This is not some diabolical plot from the cartoon world or a conspiracy theory that envisions evil geniuses plotting to take over the world. It's not even as Machiavellian as a lot of political campaigns. It's just a group of people doing what comes naturally and generating consequences that need to be addressed.

Here's how it works.

The minority who oppose self-governance are more likely to get involved in politics and government than people who view such activities as less important. In their day-to-day job activities, those who oppose self-governance naturally gravitate towards policy solutions that make sense to them. Then, like anybody else in the political world, they try to build support for their plans.

If that means playing off the partisan bickering to get something done, so be it. If it means convincing a member of Congress that a particular policy is just a minor exception to the general rule of self-governance, then that's what they'll do. And, it's worth noting, if they truly believe in government taking the lead, that's what they should do.

The end result is that self-governance needs to be defended from a group of politicos who truly want to end it. The opponents are sincere, committed, talented and pursuing their goals as part of their full-time work. This effort is both their career and their passion.

Against this political dream team are the part-time, volunteer defenders of a self-governing society. They are involved in politics only out of a sense of duty. They can't wait to finish so they can return to the real world where they can pursue their careers and their passions.

If that sounds like a tough match-up for the good guys, it is. In fact, it's very tough.

Quite frankly, there is no way that the defenders of self-governance can defeat the full-time politicos on their own. They need to find help from within the political world. Remember, Luke Skywalker won a lot of battles with his light-saber, but he didn't defeat the Emperor on his own. He won back his father and Darth Vader destroyed the Emperor.

That's why it's so important to work on redeeming some politicos who retain even a hint of respect for the concepts of self-governance.

Going the Wrong Way

Unfortunately, the politicians and their allies have spent the last century moving in the opposite direction, doing everything within their power to make voter oversight more difficult. They have created a system where all but the newest Members of Congress have more job security than a tenured college professor.

That concept, a perpetual Congress, is exactly the opposite of what the Founders had in mind when the Constitution of the United States was written. The House of Representatives was designed to be the branch of government closest to the people and a guardian of self-governance. Because keeping control of the purse strings close to the people was a common sense way to keep the people in charge, only the House was given the right to initiate tax increases.

The House, as envisioned in the Constitution, was to be filled with representatives, not leaders. An ever-changing group of people who served briefly and then did something else with their lives was expected.

The Founders wanted the House to be a boiling cauldron of new ideas, some of which made sense and others which did not. They wanted a venue for ideas and passions to enter into debate and challenge the status quo. In short, this was a place where the frustrations of the citizens could be voiced in the halls of power without careful screening by political handlers.

But the Founders crafted a careful system and also created the Senate to balance out the wild ideas proposed by the House. It was to be filled with more mature statesman who would hang around the Capitol for a while, retain institutional knowledge, and dampen down the excesses of unfettered democracy in the House. As noted earlier, the Senate was designed to keep bad bills from becoming law.

It worked pretty well for a long time.

When the Constitution was written, the Founding Fathers expected that there would typically be about a 50% turnover in the House of Representatives every single election. That's not a typo. Fifty percent (50%) turnover was the norm in Colonial America as roughly half the legislature was new every session. That kind of turnover was also the reality in the United States for most of the 18th and 19th centuries.

Politicians began to tinker with the election rules though, and during the 20th century turnover steadily declined. Many changes gave legal advantages to Republicans and Democrats to help them exclude third parties from competing. In 1968, for the first time ever, turnover in Congress fell to single digits.

Even in 1994, the year of supposedly massive upheaval that gave Republicans temporary control of Congress, 80% of incumbents returned. In 2006, when the Democrats regained control, turnover was even lower.

It's important to understand that the desirability of turnover was more than just a belief in getting new ideas into play. It was a central means of controlling those in power.

The *Federalist Papers,* written to promote passage of the U.S. Constitution, said that the best way to control members of Congress was to insure that they came back home and lived under the laws they imposed on the rest of us.

That was a common sense idea and one that the political and corporate elites have worked hard for decades to overcome.

Today, the politicians have won and the legislators never go home.

Just like gambling casinos write the rules to make sure the house always wins, politicians have written the rules so that incumbents always win. Term limits are a natural response to this and the strong public desire for such limits is further evidence that the American people today share the same instincts of those who founded our nation.

Not surprisingly, the popularity of terms limits among voters is matched by the hatred of limits by politicians, lobbyists, and activists.

But term limits may not be enough in today's world. It's far from clear that even term limits would force the politicians to leave their exalted perch and live under the laws they wrote for the rest of us. Retiring legislators just become lobbyists, hang around Washington, and earn a bigger paycheck.

As a result, the House of Representatives has been transformed from a defender of self-governance into the embodiment of the alliance between government and big business.

❖ ❖ ❖

Part III

Saving
Self-Governance

❖ ❖ ❖

What Can We Do?

Most normal people don't want to be dragged into the muck of politics any more than is absolutely necessary. They have better things to do with their lives and that's the way it should be.

But, there are times when all of us should take our turn and get involved just like we do at the Little League concession stand. Unfortunately, today's political world is far worse than any concession stand duty.

If we ever found a Little League team behaving as poorly as the Republicans and Democrats or the Congressmen and Senators, we'd probably disband the team and go home. Heck, we might even disband the entire league and bulldoze the field.

Tempting as it might be, we can't quite do that with the nation's political teams. It would be great to disband the parties, send everybody in Congress home, and start all over again. But, while it might put a smile on your face to think about that, it's not going to happen.

Instead, the nation may need a temporary surge of participation from those who have a life outside of politics and government. For a period of time, many may need to divert some attention away from other vitally important responsibilities of self-governance to fix a broken political system.

Without a strong effort by the American people, the elites will win and self-governance will come to an end.

That's an outcome too horrific to contemplate, let alone allow.

Frustrated citizens must find a way to fix what is broken so that government may once again truly enjoy the wholehearted consent of the governed. When that day arrives, the overwhelming majority of Americans will once again be able to focus on productive activity rather than enduring extended tours of duty as chaperones in the political world.

Still, while it's easy to see how a temporary jolt of involvement could restore common sense to the political dialogue, it's hard to suggest a particular course of action. About the only thing that's certain is that there's no point to playing the typical partisan games that politicians enjoy so much.

A different approach might be more natural to newly-engaged citizens. They could help lift the dialogue out of the typical political gutter by injecting a more positive tone to the discussion. The way to do that is to frame all political discussion in the broader and more uplifting context of self-governance. It's always helpful to remind the political types that self-governance is about far more than whether one politician beats another on Election Day.

As for the specifics, the best way to deal with the political world is generally the same as the best way to deal with children. It's not a question of sitting them down and making them listen, it's all about taking advantage of teachable moments.

In true self-governing fashion, the specifics will be accomplished by individuals trying things, seeking support, and learning what works. Sometimes, it may be necessary to shine the light of publicity on an inappropriate deal between government and big business. Other times, a throw-out-the-bums approach to elections might be good. Most of the incumbents will survive, of course, but even if only one or two established incumbents are defeated, it will send a message to defenders of the status quo.

Some of the best opportunities may come in primary elections where voters sometimes have a choice between candidates with experience in politics and other candidates with experience in the real world. Other things being equal, the candidate with real world experience will have a better chance of being sympathetic to self-governance.

It's also important to remember that there are roughly 500,000 elected officials in the United States including school boards, city councils, county boards, and more. That provides plenty of opportunity for citizens to get involved and make a difference.

Regardless of the details, the surge must take advantage of every opportunity to insure that the American people can be involved in the decision-making process.

And we must never lose sight of the fact that we are trying to restore a self-governing society. We are not trying to replace one group of politicians with another in a corrupt system. We are trying to clean up the system.

The last thing we want to do is create a situation where everybody has to get involved in the political games on a 24/7 basis. So, the surge must be temporary. When it's finished, we need to leave in place a system where people can once again go back to the important work of self-governance.

❖ ❖ ❖

Policies

When the auto industry was in its infancy, a research study suggested that the market for cars would ultimately be limited by the number of chauffeurs that could be trained. In that view, the market for cars would never top a million sales worldwide.

Auto manufacturers had a choice. They could either find a way to train more chauffeurs or they could make cars easier for ordinary people to drive. They chose to eliminate the need for chauffeurs, ordinary people took to the road with a passion, and General Motors became the world's largest company.

Today, our political system has a choice. We can either train a group of political chauffeurs to drive the debate or we can make it easier for ordinary people to take charge. That choice is even easier to make than finding ways to increase car sales.

While the choice is easy, there's not a top-ten list of legislative priorities to accomplish this goal. We shouldn't expect quick fixes to turn things around and resolve a problem that has been growing for a century. That's especially true when those in power don't want to fix it.

Still, there are several steps that would give the American people a decent chance to win.

One relatively simple approach would be a requirement that all legislation be posted and available to the public in final form for a week or so before a vote. This would apply not only to the base legislation but also to any proposed Amendments. Put the information on the Internet, let everybody see it, and have an informed debate.

If it's available for a full week, maybe even some of the more senior members of Congress will find time to read it.

Sure, this requirement would mean an end to last-minute legislative horse trading, but that's a good thing. Yes, it would be more difficult for politicians to slip in their pet projects, but that's okay too. There will be times when the legislative leaders can't round up the votes and will have to start the seven-day clock all over again, but that's better than passing something that hasn't seen the light of day.

In fact, with the exception of politicians and lobbyists who have something to hide, it's hard to think of why anyone would oppose this simple step towards transparency.

Another step towards transparency would be disclosure of all meetings between legislators and regulators. Who was there? What constituents were discussed? If the largest corporations are buying protection, let's see what they're buying. Anything that can be done to shed light on the meetings between the nation's largest corporations, politicians, and legislators should be encouraged.

Voters should also have the right to approve all pay increases for legislators, governors, and Presidents. This approval should be on the same ballot when people vote in general elections for those politicians and voters should get their say even if it's just a cost-of-living adjustment.

It might also be a good idea to develop a system that lets Members of Congress vote from their home districts as well as in the Capitol. You can almost picture the events around the country as Representatives and Senators watch major debates on the big screen with the people they are supposed to represent. Then, with the public watching and the party leaders unable to corner them, our elected politicians could cast their vote.

Some in DC might complain that face time and personal interaction are essential to the legislative process. They're right and that's the best reason for letting politicians vote back home. It would be an improvement if representatives could have more face time and interaction with the people they're supposed to represent and less time with other politicians and lobbyists.

Another set of reforms could address the control of the purse string arguments that led the Founders to restrict taxing authority to the House. Since the House has broken free of the checks and balances designed to keep legislators under control, a new approach must be found to bring taxpayers back into the loop.

The first could be a Taxpayer Disclosure Act to let each American know how much they pay in taxes. With this information at their fingertips, they could make more informed decisions.

Essentially, when the IRS sends back a refund or an acknowledgement of a payment, it would provide a summary of the taxpayers' total tax bill from all levels of government. This would include federal income taxes, payroll taxes, state income taxes, property taxes, sales taxes, gasoline taxes, taxes paid by the employer, and whatever else we pay taxes on. Obviously, some would be estimates. But, if businesses are routinely required to disclose all costs, why shouldn't the government? They could probably even come up with a Web site where people could follow up and get a more precise handle on what they are paying for government services.

Second, since the House is no longer representative of the people's concerns, voters themselves should assume direct control of the purse strings. All tax increases, at any level of government, should require voter approval before implementation. This is common sense and a logical extension of the rallying cry that founded the nation—"No taxation without representation."

With today's technology and communications capabilities, there is absolutely no rational reason to keep voters out of the loop on tax hikes.

Third, because politicians always like to make deals with other people's money, any special tax exemptions offered to individual companies should also require taxpayer approval. If a mayor wants to give a company a tax break to move inside the borders, let him explain to the people of his city why it's a good deal. If he can do that, the deal will get approved. If he can't, it shouldn't go forward.

These procedural changes may not sound like much, but they would completely change the dynamics of the legislative process and turn the world of politics upside down. Today's politicians and lobbyists would hate the changes at least as much as they hate term limits. That alone is a good indication of their value.

❖ ❖ ❖

Leadership

With a surge in public participation, there's a lot the American people can do to restore self-governance. Sooner or later, however, advocates of self-governance will have to find leaders that they can work with, if not believe in. A few insiders must be found who will work to welcome the American people back into the process.

This goes right back to the opening premise of the essay. The American people do not want to be governed from the left, the right, or the center. They want to govern themselves.

Such leaders will be hard to find in a political culture where candidates pretend to have all the answers and then line up fans to support them. Some of the needed leaders may already be in office but will require a lot of work before they can be redeemed. Remember, it took Luke Skywalker three full movies and countless battles before he was able to redeem Darth Vader.

Other potential leaders may get elected during the surge of public participation and will require a lot of supervision and support to keep them from slipping over to the other side. But, regardless of where they come from, advocates of self-governance will need some people on the inside to complete the restoration of self-governance.

This is not at all the same as dreaming of a white knight from outside the world of politics who will swoop in and set things right. That dream has a certain appeal to it, but it's not going to happen.

For one thing, the media will eat alive any rookie who is unprepared for the intense scrutiny of having every word picked apart and every move treated with suspicion. There is nothing like it in the business world, the faith world, the entertainment world, the charity world or the real world. Even Ronald Reagan and Barack Obama had been in politics for years before they became an overnight sensation.

Therefore, leaders must be found who have already survived the political initiation process and know how to deal with the daily news cycle in the media game. The trick is finding someone who has done that while still retaining a deeply held belief that governments derive their only just authority from the consent of the governed. This is hard to find because just about all Americans, even those with the absolute best of intentions, will be corrupted upon entering high elective office.

But many elected officials will retain at least some of their better instincts long after they've traded their first vote or met with their first regulator to "help" a constituent. In fact, most current politicians probably retain some commitment to government "for the people." But, a much smaller number are able to hang on to a belief that includes government "of the people" and "by the people."

And that's why advocates of self-governance need to remember Luke Skywalker. If even a few elected politicians can be turned into full-fledged advocates of self-governance, they can have a tremendous impact by working on the problem from the inside.

But, we should never underestimate how difficult it will be for politicians from either political party to make this switch and challenge the status quo. Think of how popular it would be for a high school kid to let the chaperones back in after the other kids have broken all the rules. Once a politician takes a firm and decisive action on behalf of self-governance, he or she could be shunned by former friends and colleagues.

And we must also recognize that when a few timid steps are taken in the direction of self-governance, the politicians will throw a temper tantrum. Children threaten to hold their breath until they turn blue and politicians will threaten to end popular programs if they don't get their way. They will also threaten other politicians who might be thinking of restoring power to the American people.

Still, we need to try. We can point out the benefits, we can lift our voices to be heard, and we can appeal to the better instincts of a politician's nature. We can point out that history will look kindly upon those who stood up for the American people against the political elite. Many times we will be disappointed but there will also be some pleasant surprises along the way. It will take an enormous amount of work to redeem even a single politician, but it will be well worth the effort.

Some politicians will naturally be drawn to the fact that a consensus exists and is looking for a leader. If they can figure out how to get in front of the parade, they'll be happy to do so. Others will like the power of a particular issue (a Presidential candidate could promise to never sign a tax increase without voter approval as part of a broader pitch to bring voters back into the loop).

Many will cynically and temporarily fall in line when they read the polls or see public protests on a particular issue. Some of these players will be more supportive when the other political team is in charge and less supportive when their party runs the shop. We should be happy and thankful when these folks support any kind of positive change. But, we shouldn't for a minute mistake their self-serving behavior for a commitment to self-governance.

But, amidst the phonies and the wavering fence-sitters, a few will be drawn back because their idealism is re-kindled. Those will become the real leaders. They will feel in their bones how vitally important it is for us to do all we can to insure that "government of the people, by the people, and for the people shall not perish."

It may be a long time before enough such leaders emerge. When they do, they will need to be supported.

In the meantime, we need to remember the message that flight attendants recite before every flight. If there is trouble and the oxygen masks deploy, adults are told to put on their own mask first before helping any children. In the world of self-governance, the adults need to take care of our primary responsibilities first before helping the politicians.

That means doing the hard work of self-governance even during a surge that demands extra time for politics. It means taking care of family, faith, home and job, pitching in with neighbors for community projects and giving generously to charities you can wholeheartedly support.

Those are the actions that make a difference and will lead to a better nation.

Beyond that, it's important to set a good example. If you believe that self-governance means much more than elections and political campaigns, act like it. Don't get caught up believing that the world will come to an end if one politician beats another on Election Day. Don't call for limited government without also calling for all the hard work needed to make communities work and help those in need.

Instead, show the world by your daily actions that self-governance in America encompasses every aspect of life and every institution of society. We are all governed by many things and many people. At the same time, we all play a role in governing others.

In this role, we can always seek to highlight the bad behavior resulting from the alliance between government and the largest corporations. Unfortunately, with the state of politics today, there will never be a shortage of examples!

But, while we do that, it shouldn't be made personal. We need to draw attention to the bigger problem. It's not that Members of Congress are evil; it's that they are doing their best to survive in a corrupt political system.

We need to take the same approach when raising questions about our largest corporations. The goal is to not to attack companies that succeed by serving their customers well. We want those companies to do well, create jobs, and add value to our 401(k) accounts. However, when companies buy protection from the government to avoid the consequences of the free market, we need to call them out.

For some, this won't seem like it's enough. There will certainly be a nagging frustration for many people who want to find the right leaders right now, but that's beyond our control. The American people can create a positive environment for self-governance, but we can't win until leaders step forward who will bring that message with them to the halls of power.

❖   ❖   ❖

The 21st Century

So, what does all of this mean in the 21st century?

More than anything else, a broader understanding of self-governance should give us hope.

At one level, the challenge facing the nation is simple. The American people must be put back in charge.

At another level, the task seems almost impossible. There are powerful and well-financed forces aligned against the very idea of letting people govern themselves. Our political system is badly broken and the unholy alliance between government and big business represents a significant threat to everything that makes America great.

The gap between Americans who want to govern themselves and politicians who want to rule over them may be as big today as the gap between the colonies and England during the 18th century.

If we had to rely on politicians to fix these problems, the outlook would be bleak indeed.

Fortunately, in America, the politicians aren't nearly as important as they think they are.

Despite the failures in the political world, two centuries of history has embedded self-governance deep into the soul of Americans from coast-to-coast. We are all "created equal and endowed by [our] Creator with certain unalienable Rights." Those rights include "Life, Liberty, and the pursuit of Happiness."

Because we can rely on our friends, our neighbors, and our nation's historic commitment to self-governance, we can be confident about the future.

The American people can defeat the political and corporate elites who want to rule over us. We can secure the blessings of freedom for our children and grandchildren.

It will take a lot of work, and a temporary surge in public participation, but there is no reason to believe that self-governance in America will be defeated by the current crop of politicians.

In U.S. history, every generation has done something to leave the nation a little better off than the way they found it. For our generation, the challenge is to give the United States a "new birth of freedom" so that "government of the people, by the people, and for the people shall not perish from the earth."

Our children and our grandchildren are counting on us.

❖ ❖ ❖

About the Author

Scott W. Rasmussen is founder and President of Rasmussen Reports, an independent media company specializing in the collection, publication and distribution of public opinion polling information.

His company provides in-depth data, news coverage and commentary on political, business, economic, and lifestyle topics at *RasmussenReports.com,* America's most trafficked public opinion polling site.

Columnist Michael Barone called Scott "one of America's most innovative pollsters." Both he and his firm have a reputation for delivering reliable, newsworthy, and actionable content.

Rasmussen speaks regularly at events and with the media, translating poll numbers into meaningful analysis and commentary about current events, underlying trends, and the questions that Americans are curious about.

Follow Rasmussen's work at *twitter.com/RasmussenPoll* or on the Rasmussen Reports Web site. If you'd like Scott to speak for your group or organization, contact the Premiere Speakers Bureau.

12617218R00050

Made in the USA
Lexington, KY
17 December 2011